EVANGELIZE
OR
FOSSILIZE

EVANGELIZE
OR
FOSSILIZE

HERBERT LOCKYER

WHITAKER
HOUSE

Unless otherwise indicated, all Scripture quotations are taken from the King James Version of the Holy Bible. Scripture quotations marked (RV) are taken from the Revised Version of the Holy Bible.

EVANGELIZE OR FOSSILIZE:
The Urgent Mission of the Church

ISBN: 978-1-62911-013-4
eBook ISBN: 978-1-62911-037-0
Printed in the United States of America
© 1938, 2014 by Ardis A. Lockyer

Whitaker House
1030 Hunt Valley Circle
New Kensington, PA 15068
www.whitakerhouse.com

Library of Congress Cataloging-in-Publication Data (Pending)

1 2 3 4 5 6 7 8 9 10 11 **ᵾᴥ** 21 20 19 18 17 16 15 14

To Dr. Will H. Houghton,

president of the Moody Bible Institute,
who personifies the evangelism of Dwight L. Moody,
whose vision brought the institute into being.

CONTENTS

PREFACE

At first sight, it might seem as if the title of this book is somewhat drastic. Can it be true that if we fail to evangelize, we will inevitably fossilize? What is a fossil? It is a relic of a former condition. While on the West Coast, I saw some fossilized trees. There they were, still resembling trees, but they were dead and cold, for natural forces had turned them into stone.

Truly there is nothing so tragic, so hard, and so icy as a fossilized church or Christian. Nothing can keep the Christian warm, fresh, and alive like evangelism. Soulwinning is a safeguard against a dead, barren orthodoxy.

That the church's expansion depends upon her evangelism is the testimony of the ages. Failing to save, she cannot survive. Lack of evangelism ultimately means extinction.

It is the sincere prayer of the writer of these pages, therefore, that the Master will be pleased to use what is written in this book to stimulate the desire of God's people to gather in the lost, lest judgment fall upon a guilty world.

Some of the messages in this book were given at the memorable thirty-second Founder's Week Conference in Chicago, Illinois, which stands out, in the opinion of many, as one of the greatest conferences ever held under the auspices of the Moody Bible Institute.

—*Herbert Lockyer*

CHAPTER 1

THE CALL TO EVANGELIZE

"And it came to pass, that, as the people pressed upon [Jesus] to hear the word of God, he stood by the lake of Gennesaret, and saw two ships standing by the lake: but the fishermen were gone out of them, and were washing their nets. And he entered into one of the ships, which was Simon's, and prayed him that he would thrust out a little from the land. And he sat down, and taught the people out of the ship. Now when he had left speaking, he said unto Simon, Launch out into the deep, and let down your nets for a draught. And Simon answering said unto him, Master, we have toiled all the night, and have taken nothing: nevertheless at thy word I will let down the net. And when they had this done, they enclosed a great multitude of fishes: and their net brake. And they beckoned unto their partners, which were in the other ship, that they should come and help them. And they came, and filled both the ships, so that they began to sink. When Simon Peter saw it, he fell down at Jesus' knees, saying, Depart from me; for I am a sinful man, O Lord. For he was astonished, and all that were with him, at the draught of the fishes which they had taken: and so was also James, and John, the sons of Zebedee, which were partners with Simon. And Jesus said unto Simon, Fear not; from henceforth thou shalt catch men."
—Luke 5:1–11

The miracle of the draught of fish is an example of the Master's way of using what was at hand to illustrate and enforce the truth that He desired to proclaim. He had power to touch life at every conceivable point and to produce spiritual lessons for the profit of His hearers. He often employed the things that are seen to explain and emphasize the things that are unseen.

Here He is shown as loving the sea. The music of the waves reached the depths within His soul. The sea was His. He made it; therefore, it obeyed Him. He could search the depths within the sea, and so He used a physical fact as a symbol to illuminate a spiritual truth. Understanding the sea, He was well able to penetrate the depths of the human heart. And so we turn to this well-known narrative, where our Lord commandeered a boat and fashioned it into a pulpit, and laid hold of a draught of fish to illustrate the possibility of taking men alive.

There are three introductory thoughts that should be emphasized before approaching the proper theme. First of all, as believers, we have the interest of the people. Second, we have the opportunity of the disciples. Third, we have the ministry of Christ.

WHAT BELIEVERS ARE GIVEN

1. THE INTEREST OF THE PEOPLE

The people pressed upon [Jesus] *to hear the word of God.*
(Luke 5:1)

That is a very suggestive phrase, meaning that the multitude pressed heavily on Jesus to hear the Word of God. By this time, Jesus' fame was firmly established, and no matter where He went proclaiming the Word of God, the common people heard Him gladly. Wherever the Lord is lifted up and exalted, there is always an eager company of people gathered together to listen to the message. When the Word is fully and faithfully preached in the power of the Holy Spirit, there is never lacking an appreciative audience.

2. THE OPPORTUNITY OF THE DISCIPLES

Christ wanted to reach the crowd. How was He to do it? Why, He used what was at hand; and so you find Him entering the boat of Simon Peter and using it as a pulpit. I wonder if He is using your equipment to extend the influence of His cause among men? The Lord is still eager to proclaim His message, but the difficulty is this—He does not have enough boats to use. Is He occupying the throne of your heart and teaching men and women out of the ship of your life? Let Him have your boat, and He will reward you with a haul of fish.

3. THE MINISTRY OF CHRIST

And he sat down, and taught the people out of the ship.

(Luke 5:3)

What a great open-air service that must have been, with an extempore sermon proclaimed from a most singular pulpit. We read that Jesus taught the Word of God to the people. He had no other message for them. As you can see by turning to the narrative, the Lord sanctified what He used. Dean Stanley said of the little lake of Gennesaret, where Jesus had been in this passage, "It is the most sacred sheet of water the earth contains"; and that is simply one way of saying that the Lord Jesus adorns everything He touches.

Perhaps you have been attracted by the phrase *"He sat down, and taught the people"* (Luke 5:3). That was the usual attitude of Jewish preachers. Ministers today stand to proclaim the Word, but the Jewish preachers would sit to declare the oracles of God; and in a real sense, the Lord Jesus has sat down on the right hand of the Majesty on high, in order to teach the multitudes out of the ship about His church.

Furthermore, as you can see, the Lord Jesus turned from the people to Peter, and thus the message chosen for our meditation was spoken to Peter as an individual. Christ's greatest work was not with crowds, but with individuals; therefore, may each of us hear His word. He is bidding Peter to launch out into the deep, and there are several spiritual deeps within the narrative, all of which we must plunge into, just as Peter did. There is a parable wrapped up in this miracle. First of all, there is the deep of failure.

THE DEEP OF FAILURE

Master, we have toiled all the night, and have taken nothing.
(Luke 5:5)

That sad confession is descriptive of the church in general today. For wherever we turn, we have an excess of denominational toil, but little or no fruit; we have plenty of toil, but no taking. Think of the energy that is poured out upon secular efforts that are unproductive of deep spiritual results—a continual grind and little to show for it.

The word *toil*, as used in this passage, is very profitable to study. In this passage, we see that the disciples did not toil laboriously; their labor was rather easy. The indication is that on this particular night, they were not caring whether they took any fish out of the lake or not. This may account for their failure, and it may be that this is the reason for our spiritual failure. There has not been enough sacrifice and surrender and tears. Our labor has been rather easy.

What days of discouragement these are because people keep finding themselves in the deep of failure! There is a spirit of defeatism abroad from which we ought to pray to be delivered. Many are on the verge of giving up and laying down their nets. I wonder if you are having that experience right now! You are conscious that you have been toiling and toiling and toiling, on the verge of resigning, for all that I know. But will you bear this thought in mind, that the resignation of a tired, discouraged worker is never valid? The Lord would have us continue at our task, no matter if we are seeing results or not. *"We have toiled all night, and have taken nothing."* Let us be honest and recognize our failure, and confess it to the Lord.

THE DEEP OF SPIRITUAL EXPERIENCE

The second deep is found in Luke 5:4, and we might name it "The Deep of Spiritual Experience." The Master said, *"Launch out into the deep, and let down your nets for a draught"* (Luke 5:4).

We turn back to this verse because it reveals the reason for the disciples' failure that night upon the lake. Those fishermen had been plying their nets very near to the shore, but the fish were not there, so Jesus urged them to push out into deeper water.

Perhaps our lives are somewhat shallow. We have been living too near to the edge of the shore, and no fish can be found there. We must push out from the shore—out into deeper blessing, out into the depths of prayer and trust and love and abandonment to the God of the sea. We must learn to dwell deeply. Are we spiritual divers, bringing up from the deep the pearls of dying souls lying on the bottom of the human sea, and landing them upon the shores of salvation and eternity?

It may be that we have been toiling and taking nothing, simply because we are not out in the deep of consecrated service. We may be too cold and formal and mechanical. Our experience may be somewhat shallow and superficial. We must learn how to be more closely identified with the work that is dear to the heart of our blessed Lord. Let us launch out into the deep. Let us surrender our nets and our ships to the God of the ocean; that is, our gifts and our abilities and our opportunities for service. Let us push out into the deep water—out into experiences of the sanctifying grace of the Holy Spirit up to this time unknown, for they that do business in deep waters are those who see the works of the Lord and His wonders in the deep.

THE DEEP OF OBEDIENCE

In the third place, you have the deep of obedience, as we see in Luke 5:5 and 6: "[Simon said] *nevertheless at thy word I will let down the net. And when they had this done, they enclosed a great multitude of fishes: and their net brake.*"

It is essential to get to the bottom of these words if we are to understand all that is contained in that act of obedience. Peter was a fisherman, and Christ was a carpenter; so Peter might have reasoned with his Lord, "Well, Master, you know all about wood and nails, but I have been at this business of fishing from my earliest years, and I know that this is not the time to fish. We go out at night, for that is the time to take fish. The glare of the morning sun on the silvery water causes the fish to hide. Jesus, this is not the time to fish!"

But though Christ was a carpenter and Peter a fisherman, Peter responded to the command of his Lord and let down the net for a draught, for Jesus was likewise the Master of ocean and earth and sky.

Should Peter have gone out and fished? Experience and reason would have told us "No," but Jesus said, "Yes, let down your nets for a draught" (see Luke 5:4), and Peter obeyed. And after he obeyed, Peter came to know that obedience is the key to God's bountiful supplies.

So we may argue that today is not the time for a revival; and there are those who discourage all thought of a quickening of the spiritual life of God's people in this day. They say to us, "Why, look at the chaotic condition of the world. See national and international unrest and disorder and the multiplication of worldly and iniquitous forces which militate against the truth. It is impossible amid the chaos of things to expect God to travel in the greatness of His strength."

But the darkness of the hour does not preclude a revival. We have every right to expect God to manifest His power in this day that is pregnant with opportunity. Faith never questions the word of God; it never argues. At Thy word—at *Thy* word—I will let down the net. It is our responsibility to obey, and it is Christ's responsibility to supply the fish. If there is absolute resignation to Him who made the spacious sea, then He will amaze us with spiritual success.

It is wonderful to realize that on that day and at that moment, the Lord knew where the shoal of fish could be found. Possibly, by His power, He brought the fish into the net of Peter, for His deity commanded all the circumstances. He was King among His own arrangements, as well as at home amid His own laws. On that day, as the Lord of nature, He revealed His dominion over the fish of the sea.

Are we willing to obey the Lord? No matter how unlikely the time and the place for soulwinning may be, if we are urged by the Spirit of God to let down our nets, then it is the Lord's responsibility to bring about the contact between the negative of human need and the positive of divine supply. No matter how the prompting of God may contradict previous experience, it is our responsibility to obey.

> Once from His boat He taught the curious throng,
> Then bade me let down my nets into the sea;
> I murmured, but obeyed, nor was it long,

Before the catch amazed and humbled me.
His was the boat, and His the skill,
And His the catch, and His my will.[1]

THE DEEP OF UNITY

*And they beckoned unto their partners, which were in the
other ship, that they should come and help them.*   (Luke 5:7)

What a delightful touch this is! They beckoned unto their
partners in the other boat. Those early fishermen were fast friends
and partners in their occupation. We hear a great deal these days
about sharing. Well, here you have sharers, for when success
crowned the efforts of Peter, he immediately called for others to
share in what the Lord had made possible. Here we have a forceful
illustration of the ideal church.

A few weeks ago, I found myself in a Presbyterian church
where it was difficult indeed to declare the Word and to gather the
people together in a unified way, because the church was cursed
with cliques—so many coteries, sections, and divisions. One
department did not want anything to do with another department. That ought not to be! The ideal church is one in which there
is a constant beckoning unto the partners, where all work together,
and where all have a common desire to reach out to others. *"They
beckoned unto their partners, which were in the other ship"* (Luke 5:7).

How does this generally work out in the church? It is often
the case that the increase of one church means the depletion of
another. I can take you to churches that have been built upon
wreckage, and because of this, they can never stand. Sometimes
when blessing breaks out in one church, and the spirit of revival is

---

1. George MacDonald, "The Boat."

abroad, friends in that community are so anxious about conserving the results that they are jealous lest others should come in and participate.

May God give us large hearts, and if blessing breaks out in your church, my brother, be willing to beckon those who are around you. What a great thing it would be if blessing broke out, let us say, in a Presbyterian church, and there was a rising of the spiritual tide, and the friends in that community called in the Baptists, the Methodists, and the Congregationalists to share in the blessing!

Truly, the greatest need of the church of the living God in these last days is the unity of the Holy Spirit. Satan knows that his time is short, and so he is having one last throw, seeking to mar the unity of God's people. John 13:35 says, *"By this shall all men know that ye are my disciples, if ye have love one to another."* As we manifest the love and unity of the Spirit of God, we are indeed partners in this great work.

You can take that word and apply it to your own makeup, as well, for all your faculties and talents and powers should be looked upon as partners. The powers of your head ought to call the powers of your heart into fuller service for your Lord.

THE DEEP OF DIVINE REVELATION

Depart from me; for I am a sinful man, O Lord. (Luke 5:8)

When the Lord manifests His power in us, we have a revelation of our own nothingness. No matter where you turn, you will find that recorded large in Holy Writ. Job witnessed the revelation of the Lord and cried, *"Behold, I am vile"* (Job 40:4). Isaiah saw the Lord high and lifted up and confessed, *"Woe is me! for I am undone; because I am a man of unclean lips"* (Isaiah 6:5). John saw the glorified Redeemer and fell at His feet as dead. (See Revelation 1:17.)

And here is Peter witnessing the display of the Lord's power, and, amazed, he exclaims, "Depart from me, O Lord, for I am a sinful man." (See Luke 5:8.) The sea may be deep, but the deepest thing in all God's universe is the human heart. And so out of the depths of his heart, Peter cried unto the Lord.

In his cry, we see a trinity in unity: humiliation, unworthiness, and confession. And that threefold cord is not quickly broken. Humiliation is seen when Peter fell down at Jesus' knees. The goodness of the Master led him to repentance. Peter now realizes that the Lord is high over all. His unworthiness is seen in his cry, "Depart from me; get out of my boat, Lord, for I am not worthy that you should stay in it." Sin ever demands isolation. Last, he confesses, "Lord, I am a sinful man." (See Luke 5:8.) There you have the reflex of this vision. Peter comes to understand that there are buried depths within his own heart that only Jesus is able to discern and understand.

That "*depart*" is not the "depart" of a will refusing the Lord, but the cry of one discovering the vileness of his own heart. Peter was very honest and came by a new way to believe in the authority and power of the Master. Peter realized that if Christ was able to see the fish in the deep sea, He could discern every sin in the depths of his own heart.

THE DEEP OF SERVICE

Fear not; from henceforth thou shalt catch men. (Luke 5:10)

Such an occupation must be a permanent one, for this phrase can be translated, "Thou shalt be catching men." From that hour, Peter went forth to function as a winner of souls. How that word to Peter was blessedly realized on the day of Pentecost, for as he plied the gospel net in one haul, he landed three thousand souls on the shores of salvation! *"Fear not; from henceforth thou shalt catch men"* (Luke 5:10), or, as we can state it, "Take them alive."

There is this difference, however, between taking fish from the sea and rescuing souls from sin. When a fisherman plies his net and takes a fish from the sea, he takes the fish out of its natural element, and it dies immediately. But when we fish for souls, we lay hold of men and women who are dead in trespasses and sins, and they are made alive through catching them. That is the import of the Master's Word, "Henceforth thou shalt take men alive." They are eager to live after you have landed them on the shores of salvation.

My brethren, let this word ring in your ears: *"Fear not; from henceforth thou shalt catch men."* You may have picked up this book discouraged; you may have labored long and hard; you may have had little results in your ministry; and you may feel crushed and defeated, on the verge of giving up and surrendering. Let this hour mark a spiritual crisis in your experience. *"Fear not; from henceforth thou shalt catch men."* If you are willing to launch out into the deep and surrender yourself anew to the Lord, He will lay hold of you and send you back to the sphere where there has been little blessing, cause you to gather in many souls, and thereby give you the joy of magnifying His name.

Peter is now prepared to work in the depths of the human heart, for he has discovered something of the depth of his own needy heart. In Peter, vision led to vocation. Do not forget that you can never function for God in your vocation unless you have a similar vision to that of Peter. *"Depart from me; for I am a sinful man, O Lord"* (Luke 5:8). Those men at that lakeside never forgot the sacred imagery of the fisherman. They went forth to function in the way the Lord declared.

"Come after me and I will make you fishers of men. I will bait your golden hook of transfigured personality with food of angels, and men shall not be able to resist your noble winsomeness."

One of the earliest hymns extant of the church, written by Clement of Alexandria, was founded on the very imagery of the fisherman:

> Fishers of men, the blest,
> Out of the world's unrest,
> Out of sin's trouble sea,
> Taking us, Lord, to Thee;
> Out of the waves of strife,
> With bait of blissful life,
> Drawing Thy nets to shore
> With choicest fish, good store.

THE DEEP OF SURRENDER

They forsook all, and followed him.   (Luke 5:11)

Last of all, we have the deep of surrender.

That is the ultimate deep of all who follow fully. Deep ever calls unto deep. (See Psalm 42:7.) Once we catch the vision and obey the command of the all-victorious Lord, we go on to deeper depths still.

Peter brought his ship to land and left it there. He surrendered his vocation as a fisherman and became a fisher of men. That day, Peter gave his boat; but the day came when Peter gave his body, for he was crucified for his Master. God may be calling some here to follow Him fully, to leave their vocation and to launch out into the deep of fuller service, to forsake all and follow Him.

But is there not a deeper truth in this word? We must forsake everything—all past sin and failure and disobedience, the glitter and appeal of the world, and all the vain things that would charm us most—to follow Him. David cried, *"Neither will I offer burnt offerings unto the* LORD *my God of that which doth cost me nothing"* (2 Samuel 24:24).

A heathen woman was once asked why she gave her child to an idol to be destroyed by a very cruel death, and the reply of that benighted soul was, "I must give my best to my god." Is our sacrifice to be less than that of a poor heathen woman? Let each of us say, "I must give my best to my God."

If, beloved, we could enclose a great multitude of fish and have breaking nets, and witness a marvelous display of His power, wherever we labor for the Lord, then we must be willing to launch out into the deep of a full and unreserved surrender to the Lord, which will be honored by the Lord Himself.

CHAPTER 2

SOULWINNING AND HOW TO DO IT

"The fruit of the righteous is a tree of life;
and he that winneth souls is wise."
—Proverbs 11:30

"And they that be wise shall shine as the brightness
of the firmament; and they that turn many to righteousness
as the stars for ever and ever."
—Daniel 12:3

If a plebiscite could be taken regarding the greatest work in the world, a variety of answers would be received. Replies would differ according to a person's outlook. The fact remains, however, that as the greatest thing in the world is love (see 1 Corinthians 13:13), so the greatest work in the world is "soulwinning." It is, indeed, the most sublime, stupendous work ever entrusted to man.

Soulwinning is different from all other vocations in that it is eternal in its implications. Its results travel beyond the grave. A person may be successful in a profession, but such ends with death; its influence and worth are only for a short period of time. Soulwinning, however, is not for mere time, but for eternity. The soulwinner works for both worlds. He carries beyond the grave the results of his blessed vocation. In fact, a soulwinner is the only person who can shine in heaven. The honors and successes of a mere business career will not be remembered in the coming world.

Seeing, then, that soulwinning is the most important of all tasks, let us think of a few essential principles which make for prosperity in such a blessed ministry.

THE WISDOM OF SOULWINNING

Solomon reminds us that *"he that winneth souls is wise"* (Proverbs 11:30). A comparison of the King James Version and the Revised Version provides us with two helpful thoughts regarding the wisdom of soulwinning.

THE WISE WINNER

"He that winneth souls is wise" (Proverbs 11:30). This rendering suggests that we are unwise if we do not win souls, for soulwinning is the highest, most profitable occupation under heaven. First and foremost, every Christian should be a soulwinner, no matter what other sphere he may fill. Material work should help to pay expenses. Money derived from an ordinary occupation should be looked upon as a means to an end.

A striking feature of such a heavenly occupation is that it is a vocation open to all. *"He that winneth"* (verse 30) and *"they that turn many"* (Daniel 12:3) prohibit restriction as to sex, age, or culture. In the economy of God, every Christian should function as a soulwinner.

When Dr. Lyman Beecher lay dying, a ministerial brother said to the aged man of God, "Dr. Beecher, you know a great deal; tell me what is the greatest of all things." His reply was, "It is not theology; it is not controversy; it is to save souls."

That we cannot engage in a wiser, more beneficent work is evident from the testimony and example of those richly blessed in such a sphere. David Brainerd, an apostle to the Indians, wrote, "I cared not where or how I lived, or what hardships I went through, so that I could but gain souls for Christ."

THE WISE WINNING

"He that is wise winneth souls" (Proverbs 11:30 RV). The Revised Version emphasizes the thought that a person should be wise in the way he seeks to win souls. Because soulwinning is the greatest possible work, it requires the greatest possible wisdom. Being the wisest work, it requires the use of the wisest means and methods. Many are repelled and lost to God due to foolish, unscriptural methods others employ to save them. We can never badger men into the kingdom. We must win souls, not worry souls. If we would *win some*, we must be *winsome*.

Satan, as an untiring, successful soulwinner, uses all the accumulated wisdom of six thousand years to beguile sinners. And if we would deliver souls out of the satanic snare, we must possess greater wisdom than the devil. Not having this wisdom in ourselves, we must relinquish our own fleshly wisdom and fancied greatness, and take what God offers. Wisdom is ours for the asking. (See James 1:5.) Christ has been made unto us wisdom. (See 1 Corinthians 1:30.) The Holy Spirit, our Guide, in seeking out the lost, is the Spirit of wisdom.

The late Professor George Smeaton of Edinburgh used to say to his students, "Gentlemen, reckon your ministry a failure unless souls are converted to Christ." And Charles Spurgeon has reminded us, "Great soulwinners never have been fools. A man whom God qualifies to win souls could probably do anything else which providence might allot him."

THE WINNER AT WORK

A worker, then, being wise through the endowment of heavenly wisdom, is enabled to win souls. *Win* is a beautiful word and is used in various connections, all of which bring out the importance of such a sacred task as that of soulwinning. We note the following illustrations presented in Scripture:

THE SNARING OF A BIRD

Here we have the idea of a trap. Guile is used to secure a rare bird. Paul speaks of catching the Corinthians with guile. (See 2 Corinthians 12:16.) To win them for Christ, he was willing to become all things to all men. (See 1 Corinthians 9:22). Sir George Williams, founder of the YMCA, learning that a godless young fellow was fond of oysters, invited him to an oyster supper and thereby won him for Christ. There are legitimate snares we can set to catch souls.

THE TAKING OF A CITY

Sennacherib, we are told, thought to win a certain place and people for himself. (See 2 Chronicles 32:1.) In a battle, the winning of a city implies skill, patience, and hardship. The English word *win*, which comes from *winnan*, means to suffer or to struggle. And all such qualities are involved in the capture of a man's soul.

THE WOOING OF A BRIDE

Isaac and Rebekah supply a fitting illustration of this aspect of soulwinning. (See Genesis 24.) A bride is captivated by affectionate, pleading words, and wooing acts. And if we would be used of Christ to win those who will be a part of His bride, we must be actuated by tender feelings.

THE MAKING OF A FORTUNE

We speak of a man winning his way through life. A fortune is his as the result of the concentration of all his powers. By dogged perseverance and the denial of legitimate pleasures, prosperity smiled upon him. If we would be wealthy in souls, there must be the readiness to sacrifice many legitimate desires. "[His] choicest wreaths are always wet with tears."[2]

THE WINNING OF A RACE

Paul was very fond of this figure. He speaks of winning Christ; that is, gaining Him as a prize. (See Philippians 3:8.) To win any race implies the idea of abstinence, self-control, eagerness, and ambition. Thus it would be if we win souls.

THE CATCHING OF FISH

The words in Matthew 4:19 *"Follow me, and I will make you fishers of men"* are akin to "taking men alive." The sport of fishing supplies many illustrations of successful soulwinning. For example, it must be studied. One must learn how to bait a hook. The fisherman must keep out of sight, lest his shadow cast upon the water and cause the fish to swim past. And if a line is used, fish must be caught one by one.

Surely, there is wisdom needed as we cast the gospel hook into the sea of human souls! As we study those we desire to win, we must adapt the message to their need. Keep self out of sight and make Christ prominent. Reach out after souls one by one. Nothing is as fruitful as personal evangelism. May each of us pray, plan, and persevere for the prize of one precious soul!

In 1878, the greatest disaster on record associated with the Thames took place near Woolwich, my birthplace. The *Princess Alice* collided in a fog with the *Bywell Castle*. She had over nine hundred excursionists on board, and more than six hundred of them perished in the dark waters. Two ferrymen were mooring their boats for the night close to the site. One heard the crash and the cries and said, "I am tired, and I'm going home; no one will see me in the fog." At the coroner's inquest, both of them had to appear.

---

2. Edward H. Bickersteth Jr., "Come Ye Yourselves Apart," 1872.

The first was asked, "Did you hear the cries?"

"Yes, sir."

"What did you do?"

"Nothing, sir."

"Are you an Englishman? Aren't you ashamed?"

"Sir, the shame will never leave me till I die."

The coroner asked the other, "What did *you* do?"

"I jumped into my boat and pulled for the wreck with all my might; I crammed my boat with women and children, and when it was too dangerous to take even one more, I rowed away with the cry, 'O God, for a bigger boat.'"

When we think of the icy waters of infidelity; the deadly indifference to things of God in the majority of educated homes; the liberty turned to license; the profligate obscenity of much in the modern world; the very few schools and colleges in the land where the simple truth of God's salvation is fully told—surely our cry must be, "O God, for a bigger boat!"

May God give us bigger boats! If multitudes are to be found in the valley of decision, we must have larger hearts, deeper compassion, and greater yearning. Indifference, selfishness, and the exclusion from a world of need taught in some professed Christian circles contradict the command of the One who enjoined His disciples to go out into all the world and preach the gospel to every creature.

THE INCENTIVE OF SOULWINNING

In every sphere, there are strong incentives urging the Christian to give himself to his appointed task. For example, the businessman's goal is most likely money or prosperity; the scientist's goal is knowledge; the athlete's goal is the prize. In like manner, there are powerful incentives in the divine task of soulwinning that urge Christians on. These are...

THE VALUE OF A SOUL

Arthur Tappan Pierson wrote, "Practical indifference as to the peril of lost souls is eating like dry rot at the very foundations of evangelistic effort." But indifference should not be ours when we remember several things regarding those who need to be won:

THERE IS THE SUPREME CREATION OF SOULS.

Being made in the image of God, all souls are His property, and it is our business to reclaim them for their divine Owner.

THERE IS THE VALUE OF SOULS.

The possessions of a whole world cannot outweigh the value of one soul in the estimation of the Creator.

THERE IS THE COSTLY REDEMPTION OF SOULS.

God and Christ have paid the highest price for the salvation of precious souls. (See Psalm 49:8; John 3:16; 2 Corinthians 8:9.)

THERE IS THE ETERNAL DESTINY OF SOULS.

Multitudes are hurrying to a lost eternity who might become heavenly pilgrims, if only we were more concerned about their salvation.

O God, to think the countless souls that pass away
Through each short moment that we live,
Destined to dwell in Heaven or groan in Hell for aye;
O stir me up, and new strength give,
And let not one pass out through death in shame and sin
That I through Thee might seek and win.

THE DIVINE EXAMPLE

It is easy to judge the importance of soulwinning work when we realize the place it has in the mind of God. Does He consider the snatching of souls from sin and destruction the greatest and wisest work that could engage His attention, as well as ours? Why did He send His beloved Son from heaven? Did He not come solely as the Savior? The angels proclaimed Him as such. His very name—Jesus—carries with it the promise of deliverance from sin. He Himself declared that His supreme mission was to seek and to save the lost. (See Matthew 18:11; Luke 19:10.) Paul, in like manner, reminds us that Christ Jesus came into the world to save sinners. (See 1 Timothy 1:15.)

Jesus was the perfect Soulwinner, as His treatment of souls mentioned in John's gospel so clearly proves. Those incomparable stories in Luke chapter 15 likewise reveal the compassionate heart of the Savior, as well as the combined effort of the Trinity to recover the lost.

THE CHURCH'S HISTORY

A careful perusal of the book of Acts reveals the early church as a soul-saving medium. Then, every Christian was a soulwinner, hence the rapid spread of the gospel in the early days of Christianity. Turn where you will in this historic document, you find those early converts reaching out after others. Andrew brings Peter; Philip finds the eunuch; and so the river flows on.

Soulwinning should be the supreme passion of the church today, for God destined her to function in all ages as the medium of evangelism. "To neglect souls is treachery to our trust and treason to our Lord. No wonder Evangelical soundness is lost, when the Church shuts her ears to the cry of perishing millions, and to the trumpet-call of her divine Captain."[3]

---

3. Arthur Tappan Pierson, *Evangelical Work in Principle and Practice* (Astor Place, New York: The Baker and Taylor Co., 1887), 34.

If the church fails to evangelize, she must fossilize. In many particulars, she is nothing but a fossil. She has her prayers but no passion; form but no force; liturgy but no love; creeds but no compassion. For her existence, establishment, and extension, the church must depend upon evangelism. Ceasing to win, she wastes; failing to save, she stagnates. *"A true witness,"* Solomon reminds us, *"delivereth souls"* (Proverbs 14:25). God grant that His church may function in these last days as a true witness! May she be true to the divine commission! "Go…Preach…Make Disciples!"

THE REWARD OF SOULWINNING

For many people, no matter what vocation they follow, the uppermost thought in their mind will be, What am I going to get out of this? When it comes to soulwinning, it is evident that such a sacred task is not only wise but most profitable, in that it yields the highest returns. Think of its reward:

TO GOD

Nothing fills heaven with such unbounded joy as the sight of souls weeping their way to Calvary. (See Luke 15:10.) To win men and women for Christ makes Him supremely happy. (See Isaiah 53:11.) May each of us live to add to His joy!

TO THE CHURCH

The only way by which we can add members to the church, which is His body, is not by giving money, distributing suitable literature, or furthering social schemes, all of which may help, but by definite, individual contact with those souls near at hand waiting to be won. Islam has spread because every Muslim is trained to be a missionary. And if every Christian would be a missionary, trying to win those beside him to the Lord, what wonderful times of revival the church would experience.

TO THE SOUL WON

We do the best for souls, not when we clothe, feed, elevate, or educate them, but when we win them for Him who died for their salvation. When we convert a sinner from the error of his way, we not only save his soul from death but cause the blood of Christ to hide a multitude of his sins. (See James 5:19–20.)

TO THE WORLD

The soulwinner does more for the world than the educator, scientist, reformer, or legislator. It is in this higher region where souls are transformed by the vision of God that problems are solved. The way to end war, abolish all kinds of evil, and elevate humanity is to save men and women. Soulwinners are a nation's most valuable asset.

TO THE WINNER

Nothing can enrich the life of a Christian like that of bringing others to a saving knowledge of Christ. Enjoined to bring forth fruit, we fulfill thereby the purpose of our divine ordination. (See John 15:16.) And in the "Great Hereafter," soulwinning secures eternal reward, for they who turn many to righteousness shall shine as the stars forever and ever. (See Daniel 12:3.). Beloved, will souls saved through your witness form your crown of rejoicing at the judgment seat of Christ? (See 1 Thessalonians 2:19.)

> Will there be any stars, any stars in my crown
> When at evening the sun goeth down?
> When I wake with the blest in the mansions of rest,
> Will there be any stars in my crown?[4]

---

4. Eliza E. Hewitt, "Will There Be Any Stars," 1897.

THE JOY OF THE SOULWINNER

Regarding the joy of soulwinning, it is but fitting to add the following message on "The Joy of the Soulwinner" by F. Spencer Johnson, as it appeared some time ago in *The Christian*.

It was Mr. Johnson who some thirty-two years ago led me to Christ. It is, therefore, with peculiar delight, that I am able to include my spiritual father's message in this meditation.

"There is joy in the presence of the angels of God"— over a great evangelistic mission? No! Over some wonderful meetings held in the Albert Hall? No! "Over one sinner that repenteth."

A minister said to me: "How is it that I can get my deacons and officers to work hard in a great evangelistic campaign, but when they come back to our church I cannot get them to do anything?" Have we not made a mistake in waiting for some big thing to come along, when all the time our work is around us—in the omnibus, in the railway train, wherever we are amongst strangers?

How many of us who have Sunday school classes, who preach, who go about doing Christian service, realize that the angels in heaven do rejoice over one sinner that repenteth? Surely, if it were clear to our spiritual vision, we should be more busy for the Master, and not be afraid of a few difficulties. Joy in heaven? Yes! but there is also joy upon earth.

We have seen joy in many a family, when the father has been won for the Lord, when the mother has been brought into the kingdom, or when the wayward son has been brought back. Let us ask God to equip us for this great and glorious work. Joy in heaven, and on earth, and in our own hearts—there is no joy on earth like this, the joy of winning souls. We are greatly privileged. Do we appreciate our privileges? Let us make up our minds that we will bring joy to somebody's heart before we go to sleep. We talk about benefitting our country, and doing something to make things better. Let us pray that God will use us as soon as He will; and then the Lord and we and the angels in heaven will rejoice at the same time.

LESSONS FROM FISHING

"Fishers of men." As boys, we used to go to a stream; we would get a stick out of the hedge, tie on the end of it a piece of cotton or strong thread, attach to this a pin for a hook, and get our bait in the field. We would be there fishing in the stream, and doing quite a big business! By-and-by we got proud, and saved our pennies, and went in for a brand-new fancy rod. It was more fancy than strong. Off we went with it to try to do something wonderful; but almost as soon as we began to fish, the end of the rod got smashed, and then the line got twisted, and the hooks got mixed up. The thing was too fancy, and altogether we made a failure of fishing.

Is not that the way with a good many Christian people? They are not satisfied with the simple method of fishing for souls. They want to get something fancy, to give out some strange doctrine, or some "sugarcoated" message, in order to win people. That is where failure comes.

A successful fisherman can give us many wise, useful little hints. "Keep very quiet; get behind a post; do not let your shadow get on the water; when you have an encouraging bite, pull up the line." As we seek to win souls, let us be hidden behind the cross, so that our personality does not intrude. Let only Jesus be seen, and then we shall not be long in winning them.

They say that when rain is coming down the fish bite splendidly. Here is a fine illustration for us. We desire to win for Christ someone living near us, and a "rainy day" comes along; there is trouble and sorrow in that home. That is our opportunity; and if we go to such a one with God's Word, with the message of eternal life, and with personal witness and Holy Ghost power, we shall do successful work for the Lord Jesus Christ. There is a great word in Luke 5:10, "*Fear not; from henceforth **thou shalt catch men**.*" Let us not tremble, let us not excuse ourselves. "Fear not; thou *shalt catch* men." Fear not; from henceforth thou shalt catch men.

GOD CAN USE US

It may be that we have been tongue-tied for years, and we want to be liberated. Let us claim our freedom, that God may use us to some poor soul who is waiting for a message through our lips—because God has chosen us to convey it to that particular person.

I cannot put the gospel to that one as you can—God has given you a way of presenting it; and if you claim the power of the Holy Spirit to do so, you will be able to lead that person into the kingdom much more quickly than you perhaps imagine. Let us away with excuses. Let us have a heart searching before God, so that the fear of man may be swept out.

How often we give our money freely, but the lips remain unsurrendered! How many of us get a knowledge of God's

Word that we may be clever! How many of us seek to know more and more of the truth, and yet we find it difficult to influence our fellow men! Oh, for the heart knowledge! *"Thy word have I hid in mine heart"* (Psalm 119:11)— hiding and storing it up, the Word of God "banked" away, which shall be used with power at the right moment. Pray for more heart knowledge of God's holy Word.

THE SECRET OF SOULWINNING

As it is in the winning of a race, where there are laws or rules to be observed by the athlete who wants to win a prize, so it is in the winning of men for Christ. He has not left the greatest work in the world to be done in any slipshod, haphazard way. Divine laws must be observed and obeyed.

Alas, we get such small returns out of our service because we put so little into it. If some Christians were as careless about their business responsibilities as they appear to be about God's work, they would quickly meet disaster. Sometimes we see boys with paper hats and wooden swords playing as soldiers in the street. God knows many of us are guilty of playing at the most supreme vocation ever known. What is the true secret of successful soulwinning? Well, mention can be made of the following:

AN EXPERIENCE OF SALVATION

We cannot win until we are won. We cannot bring unless we have been brought. We cannot be the means of saving others until we are saved. Having seen Christ for ourselves, we can say, *"Come and see"* (John 1:39). If we are converted, we can strengthen others. The curse of Christian work is the folly of many who are trying to serve the Lord without a heart experience of His grace. They are working *for* the faith without being *in* the faith. *"Examine yourselves, whether ye be in the faith"* (2 Corinthians 13:5).

A WHOLLY CONSISTENT LIFE

The *life* is the *light* of men, which means that a life fragrant with the holiness of the Master never fails to illuminate other minds. The life of the soulwinner is of paramount importance, for God is not likely to use instruments adverse to His own holy character. Bearing His vessels, we must be clean. (See Isaiah 52:11.) What we are must not contradict what we say. Trying to keep other vineyards, we must not neglect our own. (See Song of Solomon 1:6.)

A KNOWLEDGE OF SCRIPTURE

The one great weapon by which we can capture men's souls is the sword of the Spirit. If we are able to rightly divide the Word of Truth, seeking souls will not seek our help in vain. It is imperative, therefore, to know how to present the way of salvation and adapt the message of the gospel to those we meet. Suppose a sinner, conscious of his need, came to you with a desire to be saved, could you point him to Jesus?

Of course, we must believe the authority of the Bible if we are to experience the thrill of winning the lost. It is positive truth that God uses. Higher critics are never soulwinners but soul-wreckers. Modernism damns evangelism! The gospel must be presented unmixed with human reasonings, philosophy, and rhetoric. A minister of experience once said, "I preached philosophy and men applauded: I preached Christ and men repented."[5]

It is the solemn obligation of every Christian worker to master the Bible so that Christ in His fullness may be presented to lost souls.

---

5. A. T. Pierson

A PASSION FOR SOULS

Souls are not lightly won. Zion must travail before she can bring forth. If we are cold, indifferent, selfish, or at ease, we can never win others. Christ's passion and compassion for the lost must characterize us. After shedding tears over sinners, He did not rest until He had shed His blood for them. And we cannot weep for the lost without sacrificing time, comfort, and money for their salvation. What a passionate soulwinner Paul was! (See Romans 9:1–3; 10:1.) May we catch his spirit!

FELLOWSHIP WITH CHRIST

It is at the feet of Jesus that we become equipped for this all-important work of winning men. *"Follow me, and I will make you fishers of men"* (Matthew 4:19; see also Mark 1:17). Constant communion and companionship with the Master brings us into sympathy with His redemptive plan. No matter how difficult the case at hand, we can talk it over with Him. Yes, and the souls we strive to win will take knowledge that we have been with Jesus. Through our eyes, and by our words, and by our persuasiveness, the accents of His love will be detected.

DEPENDENCE UPON THE HOLY SPIRIT

As it is the Spirit's work to convict of sin, to present Christ, to regenerate the soul, and to woo and win a bride for Christ, we must ever honor Him and never supplant Him. In soulwinning work, the Holy Spirit is all in all. What a great need there is to get back to the place of absolute reliance upon the Spirit! Even in evangelism, we sometimes organize the Holy Spirit out of His sacred business. Let us never forget the solemn injunction *"By my spirit"* (Zechariah 4:6)!

Led of the Spirit, the soulwinner quickly distinguishes the difference between an opening and an opportunity. Openings are often man-made. Overzealous, many feel a rush to make them. Openings when forced are most inopportune. Opportunities, on the other hand, are God-created, and when prepared by the Spirit, they prove to be effective. It is these opportunities to win souls for Christ that we are encouraged to buy up.

THE ENDOWMENT OF THE HOLY SPIRIT

It is not our passion, prayer, and perseverance that ultimately wins souls, necessary as these are. It is not our experience, enthusiasm, education, and eloquence that produce results. Neither is it our tact, contact, or wisdom, essential as they may be. But it is the mighty unction of the Holy Spirit, as Peter proved at Pentecost. *"But ye shall receive power, after that the Holy Ghost is come upon you: and ye shall be witnesses unto me"* (Acts 1:8). Thus may we enter into a covenant with the Lord for a fresh infilling of the Spirit, that souls may be brought to the feet of the crucified and risen Christ through our efforts.

THE NATURE OF SOULWINNING

If engaged in the work of salvation, it is vastly important to carry in our minds an exalted view of such a privileged ministry. The Lord might have committed this blessed task to angels; but, no, in His condescension, He uses saved men and women to reach the lost. What, then, is the nature of this holy ministry?

TO PERSUADE A SINNER TO CHANGE HIS LIFE, MASTERS, AND DESTINY

The nature of this holy ministry involves an attack upon Satan's domain; and you cannot enter foreign territory without meeting antagonism. The keener you are to win souls from Satan to Jesus, the more intense the hatred of the enemy.

Do not Promote the Church (handwritten)

TO DECLARE GOD'S AMPLE PROVISION FOR SINNERS

A true soulwinner must never rest until those he deals with are stripped of every vestige of self-righteousness. Christ must be presented as a complete Savior, and salvation as being all of grace. (See Psalm 39:5; 51:5; Jeremiah 17:9; Romans 3:10, 19, 22–23; Galatians 3:22; 5:19–21.) And faith must be inspired, not in a passage of Scripture, although such must be believed, but in a person. While Scripture is the channel of salvation, faith must be focused upon the Christ it presents. (See Isaiah 53:4–6; John 3:16; Romans 5:8; 1 Peter 3:18.)

TO SHOW HOW GOD'S PERFECT PROVISION CAN BE RECEIVED

Under this section, the emphasis will be on faith and faith alone. Reading passages like Romans 10:9 and Ephesians 2:8–9 shows the reader that salvation requires no human addition.

Repentance and full confession of sin will need to be enforced. Key verses, such as 1 John 1:9 and Matthew 9:13 should be used. Of course, it will be necessary to urge the definite acceptance of Christ. (See John 1:12.) Repentance alone can never save.

Promote church here (handwritten)

TO REVEAL THAT WHICH ACCOMPANIES SALVATION AND PRODUCES GROWTH

Multitudes of those who are dealt with and make a profession of faith go back into the world, simply because they are not rightly guided about the requirements of the new life. Babes in Christ must be pointed to the secret of the deeper life in Him.

The necessity of assurance must be stressed. Salvation does not depend on feelings but on facts. The Scriptures John 3:36; 5:24; and 10:28 provide direction on this topic. First John 5:10 is most striking in its affirmation that we make God a liar if our emotions are substituted for faith, while 1 John 5:13 tells us how the believer may *know* that he has eternal life.

And then the need of confession before others must be revealed to the new believer. The promises found in Matthew 10:32; Romans 1:16; and 10:9–10 are useful under this head.

The daily reading of the Bible, as the great secret of strength and growth, should be emphasized to the convert. The new life requires food which is provided in the Scriptures. (See Psalms 119:11; 1 Peter 2:2.)

* Constant prayer as another means of grace must be mentioned. (See Isaiah 40:31; 1 Thessalonians 5:17; Philippians 4:6.)

One must also emphasize that the Holy Spirit is the source of all power. Christ as Savior and the Holy Spirit as Sanctifier are the two gifts that the newly saved individual has received and must recognize. (See Ephesians 1:13; 5:18.)

* Wise treatment will be necessary as one faces special difficulties. Some souls with moral problems, and others with mental problems, will be met. Many guilty of procrastination will shirk the solemn issues at stake. A Spirit-guided soulwinner, however, will know how to adapt the message to different individuals.

* To those who say that they have tried before but failed, the soulwinner must discover the reason of failure and then explain the difference between *trying* and *trusting*. (See 2 Corinthians 9:8.)

* To those who affirm that they are too far down to be saved, one must give encouragement. Tell them that there is always hope for the person who realizes his sinful condition. (See Isaiah 1:18; John 6:37; 1 Timothy 1:15; 1 John 1:7.)

* To those who fear that they have committed the "unpardonable sin" (see Mark 3:29), which is a real fear to many, explain that the very fear they exhibit is a proof of noncommittal. Insensibility

characterizes those who are hardened—not fear. Explain Matthew 12:31–32 in the light of its context, and use John 6:37—*"All that the Father giveth me shall come to me; and him that cometh to me I will in no wise cast out"*—and 1 John 1:9—*"If we confess our sins, he is faithful and just to forgive us our sins, and to cleanse us from all unrighteousness."*

To those who are afraid that if they confess Christ, they may "not be able to hold out," as we sometimes hear people say, take pains to show that when they believe, they receive Someone, not something; and that Someone is the faithful Shepherd who keeps His sheep. (See John 10:29; Jude 24; 2 Timothy 1:12.)

To those who say that they cannot give up their pleasures, pursuits, and companions, be careful to state that the first step in the gospel is not to give but to receive. Make it clear that God is not asking them to give up anything, but to receive His Son. Do not attack the idols of the unconverted. (See John 1:12; Mark 8:36; Romans 8:32; Philippians 3:7–8; 1 John 2:15–17.)

To those who procrastinate and say, "Not now, but some other time," stress the folly and peril of delay. Show them that the road of "by-and-by" leads to the town of "never." (See Proverbs 27:1; 29:1; Isaiah 55:6; Luke 12:19–20; 2 Corinthians 6:2; Hebrews 3:7–8.) The story of Felix in Acts 24 will also help you to enforce the necessity of immediate decision.

It is necessary for the soulwinner to understand the need of the soul and to present the truth accordingly. As a physician diagnoses the condition of his or her patient, so the worker must probe the conscience of the sinner. As you deal with a soul, watch his or her face and mark the tone of his or her voice, for such are often a true index of sincerity or insincerity.

And as you present the aspect of truth you feel is needed, pray for conviction to be given to that person. Remember that it is not your arguments or persuasive words but the Holy Spirit using the message that saves. It is He who convicts, regenerates, makes Christ real, imparts faith, and leads to decision; so depend upon this unceasing heavenly Seeker to capture the lost souls. We cannot *save* souls—this is Christ's work. Our sacred task is to *win* souls.

CHAPTER 3

THE PERILS OF EVANGELISM

"Lest Satan should get an advantage of us:
for we are not ignorant of his devices."
—2 Corinthians 2:11

Because of the exalted nature of evangelism, it is beset by dire perils. Great doors carry with them many adversaries, and most Christians are not alive as they ought to be to the reality of Satan's personality, activity, and subtlety. They lose sight of the fact that he is a foe to be reckoned with; that he stands out as a great antagonist of Christ, His work, and His workers. His very name—Satan, meaning "adversary"—indicates the scheming, diabolical character he possesses. Thus, with every great forward spiritual movement, there is increased satanic activity.

A hellish blockade is always a sign of prospective spiritual blessing, and so we find that the enemy persists in launching his determined attacks upon the work of the Holy Spirit. He contests every inch of ground that has been yielded to the victorious Son of God, and he strives in every conceivable way to weaken and nullify the influence of the believer.

Paul knew something of the scheming propensities of the enemy, and that is why he wrote to the Thessalonians on this wise: *"I sent to know your faith, lest by some means the tempter have tempted you, and our labour be in vain"* (1 Thessalonians 3:5). The more spiritual and intense our evangelism is, and the deeper our personal holiness, the keener the assaults and animosity of the enemy will be. And so it is my task here to indicate a few devices the enemy employs to wreck and ruin a work of grace.

One may say that if evangelism is of God, then it cannot be hindered or spoiled. But because evangelism depends upon human channels, if they fail, then God is frustrated in His plans.

SUBSTITUTION OF THE VISIBLE FOR THE INVISIBLE

The first device that should be mentioned is that of substituting the visible for the invisible. Satan seeks to have us taken up with the revival rather than with the Reviver; with the blessing rather than the Blesser; with the gift rather than the Giver. He would have us concentrate upon a movement and not upon the Master. He would have us occupied with the crowds rather than with the Christ; with converts rather than the Converter, so that more stress will be laid upon visible results and emotional effects than on the deeper work of the Holy Spirit. The present-day craze for statistics is responsible for many abortive births in the spiritual realm, and some evangelists who love crowds succumb to this temptation.

Not so long ago, while in conversation with a well-known Bible teacher and evangelist, I was anxious to know something about his mode of operation. He told me that whenever he receives an invitation to minister to a certain community, he first tries to find out how many people there are in the community. Then he takes down the denominational handbook of the church from which he has received the invitation, and tries to find out how many members there are in that particular church and how much they give to foreign missions. Then, if the membership is sufficiently large and the donations of the people are liberal, so that he feels he will have a good offering, he takes that as the Lord's will that he should go. What a shame! What low standards! What base motives!

We cannot journey far with God unless we are saved from numbers. It is sadly possible to think more of the crowd than of the Christ, who in the days of His earthly ministry went not only to the cities but to inconspicuous places, proclaiming the Word of Life.

Furthermore, it is necessary to distinguish between evangelism and revival, between a mission and a revival. A mission is gotten up, but a revival is prayed down; and so there may be a mission without experiencing a revival. It is somewhat easy to organize a mission. One could carry through a mission in every city and town of this great land quite successfully by the employment of certain means. A slogan for the mission is "Organize." The keyword for a revival is "Agonize." You cannot organize a revival, for a revival comes when we are willing to lean less upon the visible and depend more upon the invisible.

The church is loaded with organization. She has organizers in abundance but a sad lack of agonizers. And yet more is accomplished through agonizers than organizers in the church of the living God. If you have one or two dear souls in your church whose knees are covered over with calluses because of their intercessions, I know only too well that your ministry is a fruitful one.

The early church knew how to agonize. That is why she had power to turn the world upside down. But gradually, she ceased to agonize and started to organize, and so in the days of Emperor Constantine, the church as an organization was achieved. But, alas, she has lost her travail pains. One may protest that it is not necessary to exercise such soul travail over the condition of men and women in their sin, thinking instead that we may pray quietly. But the testimony of the Word and of those who have been mightily used of God is this: Souls are won only as heaven is stormed. When Zion travailed, she brought forth fruit, and men and women were brought into closer conformity with the image of the Master.

Have you read the story of William Burns, the apostle to China, who, before his departure, was a flaming evangelist in Scotland? What a passion for souls he had! One day, while he was walking down Argyle Street in the city of Glasgow, he was overcome with the thought of the multitudes hurrying up and down that busy street, and who seemed to have no regard for God or divine things. He broke out into sobs, and, rushing up an alley (or a "close," as they call it in Scotland), he fell on his knees and cried, "O God, these perishing souls break my heart!" I tell you, if we knew something of that travail of soul, we would be delivered from the merely visible; and whether we have few or many souls before us, we would continually labor for the glory of God.

TOO MUCH PUBLICITY

Another peril is that of too much publicity. Publicity has been the death of many deep works of the Holy Spirit. One day, our Lord cleansed a leper and said to him, "Now, go home to thy friends and say nothing about this matter." (See Mark 1:44.) But we read that the leper went out and blazed abroad the matter, insomuch that Jesus could not openly enter into the city, and all unconsciously the leper by his publicity hindered the work of the Lord. (See verse 45.) Often, inflated press reports and exaggerated articles in religious magazines are simply "white lies." The testimony of evangelism all down the ages is this, that the less we court publicity, the purer the work of the Lord. We must be very careful how we use the world's bible—namely, the newspaper—as a medium. Of course, there is a legitimate advertisement and publicity.

Here we are meeting under the auspices of the Moody Bible Institute, the greatest institute of its kind in the world, and my association with it has caused me to realize that it has not only been one of the greatest publicity departments which institutions of this order possess, but that it is shot through with prayer and definite waiting upon God for guidance and direction. What I have in my mind is the tendency of some to rush into print and public notice as soon as something happens, simply for the sake of self-exaltation and self-aggrandizement. A volley of reports is shot at the public, so that evangelists may have a continual round of engagements. The only report that will matter in the long run is the one to be read at the judgment seat of Christ; and then it may be that the most unadvertised worker and work will stand out as the most conspicuous.

NEGLIGENCE OF INNER SPIRITUALITY

Another device of the enemy is that of negligence of inner spirituality. How subtle Satan is, and how he strives to get workers to be so busy in so-called Christian work that they neglect the spiritual fuel that maintains the fire of revival! And what is the use of our unsparing efforts and tireless activities if we lack that inner power that makes our service fruitful? If a person depends on his reputation as a preacher or a teacher, and not upon the spiritual forces responsible for any eminence he has achieved, then he is setting himself up for a fall; for a man may possess popularity and be destitute of inner spiritual power. Nothing can substitute for the wonderful secret and satisfaction and power of personal devotion to the Master, and frequent waiting upon Him for the renewal of strength and grace.

Evangelism ever makes extra demands upon those who engage in it. It is a greater tax upon one's time; it adds preparations because of a multiplicity of meetings; and if workers are not careful in the realm of evangelism, they become as a shell without a kernel. The work so dear to the heart of our blessed Lord brings the tendency to neglect the personal means of grace. When this happens, His servants become powerless, mechanical, and empty. Evangelists wish to keep up the outer machinery, but they often neglect the inner power. *"And as thy servant was busy here and there, he was gone"* (1 Kings 20:40). No matter how gifted a person may be or how intense his enthusiasm for the work of the Lord, no matter how versatile or how eloquent he may be, if his inner life is barren, then he is only as a sounding brass and a tinkling cymbal.

It seems to me, as I survey the field, that we need much more foundational living with our fundamental witness. For there is the temptation to function merely as waiters, coming to the Bible trying to find a suitable message, and then going before the people to deliver what we have discovered. We can never function as true witnesses unless we first of all look upon ourselves as guests.

I went into a certain hotel for a meal not so long ago, and the dining room was closed. I found the waitresses sitting at a table feeding themselves before they began feeding others. God save us from merely functioning as waiters and waitresses! May we first of all sit as guests at the divine table and feed ourselves; then we can feed others with the finest wheat! Indeed, the peril facing all who engage in the work of evangelism is that of the neglect of their inner spirituality.

During the last Great War, the ditty "Keep the Home-Fires Burning" used to be sung in the old country, as well as in the United States, and it was upon the lips of the soldiers as they went into battle. We can never be victorious in satanic warfare unless we keep the home fires burning. God grant that the fire of devotion, that our hearts and minds may never die out. There is no more solemn word than this in Holy Writ: *"They made me the keeper of the vineyards; but mine own vineyard have I not kept"* (Song of Solomon 1:6). The more popular our work, the more determined our purpose should be to guard our inner life. *"Lest Satan should get an advantage of us: for we are not ignorant of his devices"* (2 Corinthians 2:11).

WORSHIP OF MAN

Another peril of evangelism is the worship of man. The leaders of great movements, outstanding preachers and evangelists, are beset by many pitfalls. They have to be very careful, for all eyes are focused on them. And if a man is somewhat attractive, blessed with a fascinating personality, and has the power to influence multitudes, he is often sought after rather than the Master. There is always tragedy where the work of the Lord revolves around a personality who has a commanding appearance. Sometimes, men of this order are open to the worship of silly women.

I remember a Scotch town some years ago, to which there came a preacher with a very fascinating personality. The whole town was stirred, and while he was there, many of the women purchased pictures of him, and some were so taken with him that they put his picture beneath their pillows at night. That is not a story but a fact. Is it not tragic when the interest revolves around a human personality rather than around the Lord of glory?

The human element looms so largely that the preacher is in peril. If he is conscious of a God-given possession that attracts attention to him, he may have the tendency to draw the focus of the people to his gifts rather than to the One who made them possible. But the Lord is ever just. He will never give His glory to another; and if He gives any measure of responsibility in His work to any man, the word *"And when they had lifted up their eyes, they saw no man, save Jesus only"* (Matthew 17:8) in the transfiguration scene of the Lord should ever be before him.

SUPERFICIAL PERSONAL DEALING

Another peril in evangelism is that of superficial personal dealing. The divine method has ever been the proclamation of the

Word of God in all its fullness, the willingness of men and women to hear that Word proclaimed, and their acceptance of it. *"Faith cometh by hearing, and hearing by the word of God"* (Romans 10:17); and that order is never changed. Therefore, it is imperative to proclaim the message in a clear and definite fashion.

There has been too much mass-productive work in the realm of evangelism, and yet one does not belittle mass evangelism. How can he, when the story of Pentecost is recorded in God's infallible Word? Wherein was the value of those mighty campaigns conducted by Dwight L. Moody in America and Great Britain? God gave him the masses, but his work was greatly blest of God because he saw to it that alongside every seeking soul, there was a personal worker with an open Bible. Some of the most outstanding workers in Christian service today are those who were led to Christ in an inquiry room by personal workers who knew their Bibles. The work of the Holy Spirit in evangelism is something deeper than signing cards in a wholesale fashion.

Several years ago, I was asked to take charge of an inquiry room. A certain evangelist was coming to the city. Knowing something of his methods, I refused and received a good deal of criticism. But when the mission was over and some of those dear men in the community were receiving hundreds of cards (for some of the most consecrated Christian workers had signed decision cards creating mass confusion) and did not know what to do with them, they came to see that I was right in withholding my support for the campaign.

Unless we can have those about us who know the Word of God, and who can apply it to the personal difficulties and needs of those who are seeking the Lord, we will not get very far. There would not be the terrible backwash in some evangelistic campaigns if seeking souls were brought to the Savior by means of personal dealing instead of being urged immediately to sign cards.

There is a superficial dealing with souls of which we must guard ourselves against. We sin against God if we treat this matter lightly. We must learn to handle the sword of the Spirit, *"lest Satan should get an advantage of us: for we are not ignorant of his devices"* (2 Corinthians 2:11).

JEALOUSY

The last peril that we must guard against is jealousy. As so much depends upon Christian workers, it is necessary for us to be delivered from those petty things that hinder our influence. But alas, too often, jealousy works among those who are prominent in the evangelistic field, and consequently, they are shorn of spiritual power. Have you ever pondered the lament of that peeved, rejected Saul: *"They have ascribed unto David ten thousands, and to me they have ascribed but thousands"* (1 Samuel 18:8)? And we go on to read that from that day forward, Saul eyed David. Do you know what it is to be eyed by some jealous soul? When your back is turned, does he cast a javelin at you? Well, when you are conscious of that, and you find yourself up against the criticism and the jealousies of others who have a similar position, what do you do? Do you take up the javelin that is thrown at you and hurl it back?

I stand in fear of jealousy. It crucified my Lord. It sent Him to the cross. Out of envy, the Jews crucified Him. What if somebody else has a greater popularity and is always in the limelight and seems to be in constant demand and is forever before the public eye! Well, if that brother can preach the gospel in a better way than I can, he cannot preach a better gospel. And if, instead of criticizing him and revealing a jealous mind toward him, I surround him with my prayers and intercessions, and pray that God may keep him humble and get the utmost glory out of his ministry, I shall share in the reward for the work done at the judgment seat of Christ because I had a part in producing it. But of this we are confident: God can never use a jealous-minded preacher or teacher of the Word. It is a positive hindrance to blessing and a peril that we have to face.

If our lives are to tell for God, there are two guiding principles that must ever be kept in mind. First of all, we must always labor for the glory of God. Any lesser motive will damage our influence. The glory of the Master must be our supreme objective.

Next, we must maintain personal fellowship with the Lord Jesus. *"Without me ye can do nothing"* (John 15:5) is His solemn statement. When I arrived three years ago for my first visit to the States, the representative of the Moody Bible Institute met me in New York and handed me what he called a "clergy permit." When I went to the station and stood before the window to turn in the coupon, I was attracted by this sentence on each coupon in the permit: "Not good if detached." And so our Lord has said, *"Abide in me, and I in you. As the branch cannot bear fruit of itself, except it abide in the vine; no more can ye, except ye abide in me"* (John 15:4). And we are bound to be unfruitful if we are detached from Him, no matter how clever and gifted we may be. We must maintain personal communication with the source of all strength and grace.

Then we must seek the constant infilling of the Holy Spirit, for the Spirit of God is the Spirit of power, and He alone can make us function as fruitful branches of the vine. May God wean us away from the visible to the invisible, and make us more dependent upon the Holy Ghost, who is able to accomplish great and mighty things!

Spiritual intuition, whereby we can immediately detect the difference between what is false and the true, is another requirement. Spiritual perception is certainly needed in Christian circles today.

Then, too, we must immediately shun and suppress all thoughts of self-advantage and self-advertisement. In God's work, we must be strangers to duplicity and wire-pulling and politics. We must "lay in dust life's glory dead."[6]

And last, but by no means least, we must keep before us the final goal—the judgment seat of Christ, where all our service is to be rightly valued and rewarded.

---

6. George Matheson, "O Love That Wilt Not Let Me Go," 1882.

CHAPTER 4

THE IDEAL EVANGELIST

"Watch thou in all things, endure afflictions, do the work of
an evangelist, make full proof of thy ministry."
—2 Timothy 4:5

While D. L. Moody will go down in history as a Christian educator and a Bible teacher, he was essentially an evangelist. He was preeminently a soulwinner. Consumed with a passion to evangelize, Mr. Moody suffered nothing to turn his feet from his God-given course.

It has been said of Martin Luther, "Heaven shook a monk, and the monk shook the world." It is likewise true that God shook Moody, the boot salesman, and in turn, he shook two continents with his evangelistic fervor. And this is ever the divine way. God, first of all, finds and fashions an individual, and then through him, Christ draws the world to higher things. Do you ever wonder whom God is going to use next? Who knows? It may be you.

As an evangelist, D. L. Moody made full proof of his ministry. He approximated to the ideal, seeing that he had—

A deep experience of the grace of God;
Carried the evident mark of separation from the world;
Cultivated holy intimacy with heaven;
Was obedient to the voice of the Holy Spirit;
Shared his Master's passion for souls;
Was saved from all ulterior motives;
And labored in the light of eternity.

Several writers have sought to outline the characteristics or qualifications of an ideal pastor or evangelist. Here is a choice description by Bishop Ken:

> Give me the priest these graces shall possess:
> Of an ambassador the just address,
> A father's tenderness, a shepherd's care,
> A leader's courage which the cross can bear,
>
> ...
>
> A fisher's patience and a labourer's toil,
> A guide's dexterity to disembroil,
> A prophet's inspiration from above,
> A teacher's knowledge and a Saviour's love.

One of the most classic and appealing descriptions, however, is that given to us in the *Pilgrim's Progress*. Christian, you will remember, entered the House of Interpreter, where many profitable things were shown to him. Among the possessions fascinating Christian was that of a picture of a very grave person. And by the light of a candle, Christian noticed the sixfold fashion of the picture: the eyes of the man were lifted up to heaven; the best of books was in his hand; the law of truth was written upon his lips; the world was behind his back; he stood as if he pleaded with men; and a crown of gold hung above his head.

In his delineation of Evangelist, John Bunyan desired to portray the ministry of Mr. Gifford, whose passion for souls led him to work untiringly for the Bedford tinker. And truly, Mr. Gifford's portrait is a true description of all those whom God calls and qualifies for the supreme task of evangelism.

A PASSION FOR PRAYER

"Eyes lifted up to heaven." (See John 17:1.)

Prayer must ever be placed in the forefront. Without it, although one may be clever, versatile, and eloquent, he is only as sounding brass and tinkling cymbal. Outer fruitfulness and influence can never rise above the level of one's personal prayer life.

The early church prayer was of paramount importance. "*We will give ourselves continually to prayer, and to the ministry of the word*" (Acts 6:4). Somehow we have reversed the order. Thus, we give more time to the ministry of the Word than we do to intercession. When the church restores its apostolic emphasis on prayer, then apostolic results will be hers.

Noticing that the eyes of the very grave person were raised toward heaven, Christian asked the Interpreter, "What means this?" And the reply was, "The man whose picture this is, is one of a thousand. He can beget children, travail in birth for children, and nurse them himself when they are born."[7] A birth pang for souls, then, is born of prayer. When Zion travails, she brings forth!

There is further and deeper truth, however, to be gleaned from this uplifted gaze. As it's been said before, we must bear our great commission in our look. Is this true of us? Does our very mien indicate that we are true soulwinners? A careless, flippant look or manner will not impress the lost with the reality of the eternal. Our very deportment ought to suggest the Master we serve.

> He bore his great commission in his look;
> But sweetly tempered awe, and softened all he spoke.
> He preached the joys of heaven and pains of hell,
> And warned the sinner with becoming zeal;
> But on eternal mercy loved to dwell.[8]

---

7. John Bunyan, *The Pilgrim's Progress* (New Kensington, PA: Whitaker House, 1973, 1981), 35–36.
8. Imitated from Chaucer, John Dryden, "The Character of a Good Parson."

A PASSION FOR SCRIPTURE

"The best of books [was] in his hand."[9]

This second feature follows in natural order, for no one can have a passion for prayer without experiencing a corresponding passion for the Scriptures. The one reacts upon the other. One passion feeds the other.

But do we share Bunyan's estimation of the Bible? Is it one of the best, or is it the "best of books"? Do we believe that the Scriptures stand out as a Book among books, as the Lord Jesus does as a Man among men?

Are we not suffering from a deteriorated value of the Word? Not that the Bible has ever lost any of its intrinsic value, but the attitude of man regarding it has changed.

And further, we can never function in the realm of evangelism unless the Word is in our hands continually. There must be that daily, prayerful, and systematic study of the Scriptures if power is to be ours in the winning of souls. To a very ardent recruit about to enter the ministry, a seasoned pastor wrote, "You are quite right to trust God with your work; but remember that it was beaten incense that was used for the service of the sanctuary." And we must have more *beaten* incense. No pain, no gain!

The best of books says that we must read it perseveringly. Its gold is not on the surface; we must dig for it with the spade of prayerful study and diligent search.

If our sacred task is "to know and unfold dark things to sinners,"[10] then serious and systematic meditation must be ours. The Bible contains a complete revelation of God, and it takes the whole to interpret a part. This is one reason why we cannot read

9. Bunyan, 35.
10. Bunyan, 36.

the Scriptures as we read any ordinary book. May the God of the Book deepen our passion in this direction!

A PASSION FOR SPIRITUALITY

"The law of truth was written upon his lips."[11]

This third characteristic feature is capable of a twofold application. First of all, there must be a passion for confession. The best of books within our hands is of little use unless it breathes the law of truth written on our lips. The Word read and studied must be preached. We must strive to proclaim Christ's atoning work and justifying redemption. Our lips must be vocal with praise concerning His power to save.

The law of truth on the lips will also indicate the necessary passion for spirituality. It will be observed that John Bunyan designates the Bible as "the law of truth."[12] Surely this implies that the preacher, teacher, or evangelist must be clear and transparent in all things. Lips bearing the imprint of truth will not be guilty of lying and gross exaggeration. Neither will such lips be used in gossip or idle speech. Our lips and life will harmonize with the Word of Truth. Like as of old, the Word dwells in men. (See Colossians 3:16.) As sinners see the Word lived out in Christians, they are attracted to the feet of the Master. (See Matthew 5:16.)

A PASSION FOR SEPARATION

"The world was behind his back."[13]

The next feature arresting the attention of Christian, as by the light of the candle that the Interpreter held to illuminate the

11. Bunyan, 35.
12. Ibid.
13. Ibid.

picture, was that of a representation of the world behind the person's back. By this, Bunyan was trying to illustrate the teaching of 1 John 2:15—*"Love not the world, neither the things that are in the world."*

Pointing out this attitude, Interpreter said to Christian, "[This is] to show thee that [he slights and despises] things that are present, for the love that he hath to his Master's service."[14]

Is the world behind our backs? Have we learned that we can influence the world for God only as we die to its pleasures, pursuits, and sin-tainted methods of enjoyment? If we accommodate ourselves to the standards of the world, the day will come when our warning will be spurned, even as the Sodomites mocked Lot. The more detached we are from the ways of the world, the greater our spiritual influence over those whom we seek to win for the Savior.

Can you imagine an ungodly person who is concerned about eternal things going to a preacher or Christian worker who is worldly and carnally minded in life and outlook? Do you think a soul conscious that the end is near and that eternity is at hand would send for a minister who fritters away his time hankering after the beggarly elements of the world? Never! Instead, he would seek the advice and comfort of a separated person.

The tragedy of so many professing Christians—yes, even of some preachers and evangelists—is that the world is not *behind* their backs but *on* their backs. Instead of being crucified to the world, they coddle and caress it. And they seem to be blind to the fact that complete separation spells power for God. The Holy Spirit is ever limited in His operations when He has a worldly minded believer to work through. May we have grace to live with the world behind our backs—that is, where it can't be seen!

14. Bunyan, 36.

A PASSION FOR SOULS

"[He] stands as if he pleaded with men."[15]

Still looking at the picture of the very grave person, Christian noticed the earnest, passionate attitude of the figure portrayed. With hands outstretched, he sought the salvation of others. He stood as a dying man pleading with dying men and women to repent and turn to the Savior.

And all previous passions find their expression in this passion for souls. No one can have a passion for prayer, Scripture, spirituality, and separation, and remain indifferent toward the lost.

What Bunyan depicts here recalls the yearning of Jesus over Jerusalem. Sitting there on that green sward, looking out over the city, He gave a sob of unwanted love. The sins of the city caused Him to shed His tears and ultimately shed His blood.

Do we share the Master's passion for lost souls? Are we ambassadors, beseeching men in Christ's stead to be reconciled to God? Christ cannot be here in person, for He is at the right hand of the Majesty in the heavens; but He has commissioned us to act on His behalf. Are we failing Him? It is perfectly true that Christ alone can save souls, but He does not save them alone. He condescends to use those who are saved, hence the necessity of sharing His passion.

Can it be that these lines are being read by an evangelist who needs to have his passion for souls intensified? Accustomed to handling sacred things, you have become cold, mechanical, and formal. Love is not burning on the altar of the heart. You have succumbed to the deadening effect of familiarity. God grant that you may never become used to the thud of lost souls, as they march on to a Christless eternity!

---

15. Bunyan, 36.

Yet, must we not confess that there are times when we stand before sinners virtually unconscious of their terrible need and doom? We forget the eternal misery awaiting them if they die in their sins. Oh, may we ever realize that like Aaron of old, we stand between the dead and the living; and if the plague of sin is to be stayed, we must share the passion and compassion of the Redeemer! Yes, and the only place where this passion can be cultivated is at the foot of the cross. One cannot live at Calvary and remain indifferent concerning the lost.

A PASSION FOR REWARD

"A crown of gold did hang over his head."[16]

The diadem hanging over the head of the very grave person was the last feature of the picture to impress Christian. Did Bunyan have Revelation 3:11—*"Behold, I come quickly: hold that fast which thou hast, that no man take thy crown"*—before him when he added this item of a crown?

Explaining the crown, Interpreter said, "He is sure in the world that comes next to have glory for his reward."[17] Later on in his allegory, Bunyan depicts the man with the muckrake who could look no way but downward, yet over his head was a celestial crown.

All passion grows by what it feeds on. If, therefore, we live in the light of eternity, all previous passions referred to will be fed and developed. Let the golden crown ever be before us. Let the judgment seat of Christ with its review and reward be our constant incentive.

---

16. Bunyan, 35.
17. Bunyan, 36.

We cannot certainly work for heaven, but we can labor for our position in glory. Rewards have to be won. Will a full reward be yours? Faithfulness is to be the basis for reward in eternity. Revelation 2:10 says, *"Be thou faithful…and I will give thee a crown of life."* Reward is to be ours, not for fame, but for fidelity; not for success, but for sincerity; not for the quantity of our work, but for the quality of it. May the Master's "well done" be your portion and mine!

"Now," said Interpreter as he finished explaining the picture to Christian, "I have showed thee this picture first, because the man whose picture this is, is the only man whom the Lord of the place, whither thou art going, hath authorized to be thy guide in all difficult places thou mayest meet with in the way."[18] Let this last thought linger in the memory! "Authorized to be thy guide"! Are we authorized guides? Clever, popular, attractive, and eloquent though we may be, yet we are utterly deficient as safe guides when seeking souls come to us inquiring the way to God's country.

The ideal soulwinner, then, is the one who answers to the six-fold qualification: eyes lifted up to heaven; the best of books in the hand; the law of truth written upon the lips; the world behind the back; standing as if pleading with souls; and a crown of gold above the head.

---

18. Ibid.

CHAPTER 5

JONAH THE EVANGELIST

"Arise, go to Nineveh, that great city, and cry against it."
—Jonah 1:2

What a remarkable book Jonah is! In some respects, it is the most dramatic book in the Bible. It is certainly a book which every evangelist and soulwinner should read. A man with power to shake a city of some 750,000 souls should surely command our attention. Jonah was able to preach to the Ninevites, and they responded in an attitude of repentance—from the king down to the humblest servant. There must be something about his life and ministry that stimulates us to walk in more effective service.

As a spiritual giant, Jonah pushed back the waves of legalized and universal sin, pitted himself against established idolatry, and triumphed alone—yes, alone with God. What was the secret of his power? How came Jonah to be the important figure he was in an unprecedented revival?

There is much that could be written on the book of Jonah. Its historical and prophetical value is incalculable, while the lessons to be gleaned are among the deepest that one can learn.

Modern critics affirm that both the book and the person of Jonah form a combination of allegory and myth, but this question of Jonah being an historical personage is forever settled by the declaration of our Lord:

For as Jonah was three days and three nights in the belly of the whale [sea monster]; so shall the Son of man be three days and three nights in the heart of the earth. The men of Nineveh shall stand up in the judgment with this generation, and shall condemn it: for they repented at the preaching of Jonah; and behold, a greater than Jonah is here.

(Matthew 12:40–41 RV)

The sole reason for the wide rejection of the historical accuracy of Jonah is the miraculous element in the book. But when one accepts the omnipotence of God, he has no difficulty believing the book to be true history. Earlier Jewish sources confirm this viewpoint.

Jonah possessed a befitting name for one commissioned of God to bring a great, sinful city to repentance. "Jonah" means "dove," and all who serve the Lord as soulwinners must know how to mourn as doves over the sins and sorrows of the world. They must likewise be as harmless as doves. (See Matthew 10:16.)

Coming to the purpose we have in mind in associating Jonah with successful evangelism, let it be at once stated that power is ever linked with human character. The results of revivals depend upon the lives of those who engage in it. An influence such as what Jonah exerted is the invisible, indefinable force of a consecrated life. Fruitful service is never independent of the moral nature of those who serve. God is ever ready to supplement our weakness, but He would never condone our sin. Impurity robs the worker of power. It was Robert Murray McCheyne who declared, "It is not great talents that God uses, so much as great likenesses to Jesus. A holy man is a mighty weapon in the hands of God."

MARKS OF DEATH AND RESURRECTION

The solemn warning that the people of Nineveh heard from Jonah's lips included something more than mere mental force and eloquent delivery; in it, there was the evident mark of a God-sent message. Many fail in delivering God's Word, not through any lack of oratory or zeal, but because of the absence of integrity and sincerity. They forget that the *life* is the *light* of men. The fact that a Christlike character is more important than any intellectual equipment has somehow been forgotten.

Here, then, is the secret of Jonah's successful mission in Nineveh. He could enter the city as courageously as if an army of warriors were behind him, seeing that he bore, branded upon his deportment, the unmistakable stigmata of fruitful evangelism—namely, death and resurrection.

What happened to Jonah in the belly of the great fish, which was divinely prepared to receive the runaway prophet? To our way of thinking, he actually died and rose again, thereby becoming a striking type of Christ's death and resurrection. It was thus that Jesus spoke of Jonah as a sign. (See Matthew 12:39.)

God kept His servant alive within the sea monster, in spite of inward heat and the possibility of suffocation. But however miraculous it was that he was kept alive for three days, there could not have been a better example of Christ who died and was buried for the same length of time. If Jonah did not experience a death and resurrection, then there seems to be a lack in our Lord's reference to Jonah as a sign of His physical death and bodily resurrection.

The grim figure of the prophet, crying with a piercing voice and bearing the marks of death and resurrection, struck terror in the hearts of the Ninevites. Jonah was a sign of God's mercy through substitutionary death and resurrection. He was presented as a figure of atoning death on behalf of Nineveh and a sign of the loving, merciful presence of the dying One.

Promptly, upon penetrating the metropolis, Jonah announced God's ultimatum. And the appearance of a man from his unique grave, bearing such a startling and terrifying message, moved the city to repentance with compelling force. The report of Jonah's entombment and deliverance was possibly carried to Nineveh by the mariners. Seeing that the "fish" was the god worshipped by the Ninevites, the fact of Jonah dying within a fish, yet resurrected out of such a watery grave, compelled them to listen to his message of judgment. The truth that Jesus emphasized when He referred to the mission of Jonah was that the Ninevites repented at the preaching of a dead and risen prophet, but that Jerusalem would not repent even though they were warned by a dead and risen Messiah.

Why have I labored to make this aspect of the book of Jonah clear? Well, the application is clearly evident. The evangelist or soulwinner can only count for God when he, like Jonah, bears the evident marks of death and resurrection. Christ Himself was not preached to the great Gentile world until after the death and resurrection of His body; hence, His mystic word about the grain of wheat falling into the ground and dying, and through death and resurrection producing a glorious harvest. (See John 12:24.)

IDENTIFICATION WITH CHRIST

Jonah had to die and rise again. Christ had to die and rise again. That same body that was placed in Joseph's tomb had to come out again. And if we would have a message that will spread like wildfire and command repentance, we, too, must live and labor as men who have died and risen again.

Brother, have you died with Christ? Is there a grave somewhere in your pilgrimage in which you have laid "in dust life's glory dead"[19]? Or is the self-life too prominent? Although you may be a Christian seeking to serve the Lord, are you still self-centered? Self-dependence, self-effort, self-glory, self-aggrandizement, and

---

19. Matheson, "O Love That Wilt Not Let Me Go."

self-advertisement are traits that cripple the power of every soul-winner. Death to self, sin, carnality, and worldliness, and a daily death, are ever the first halves of successful evangelism. The other half is resurrection, a constant realization and appropriation of the risen, glorified, throne life of Christ.

Jonah rose again! Is the risen life of Christ yours? Do you know what it is to rise from your dead self to a higher, more blessed life? The life of self is death! The death of self is life! Is such a life the one that drives your message home? Judicially, of course, you have been raised and made to sit with Christ in the heavenlies; but after having been risen with Christ, is there the manifestation of the power of His resurrection in you and in your ministry?

Here, then, is the sign for which a guilty world waits! And repent it will when more of those who proclaim the gospel carry conspicuous signs of death and resurrection. Jonah preached the shortest, most pointed revival sermon ever proclaimed; yet it produced the greatest results, proving that it is not the length of the message that tells, but the quality of both the message and the messenger.

Had Jonah gone to Nineveh with a review of the latest book or novel, or a sermon on some passing event or scientific discovery, the city would have never been shaken. As a solitary stranger, he thundered out the stern, plain, short message of judgment—a judgment tempered with mercy, seeing that forty days of grace were granted. Coming from his watery grave, breathing the balmy air of resurrection, Jonah's witness stirred the city out of its pollution. He spoke to a dying, doomed people as a man raised from the dead.

CALL TO REPENTANCE

Let us try to picture this risen one going through the streets among the merchants in the market places, into the haunts of sin and up the palace steps to the king, crying, *"Yet forty days, and Nineveh shall be overthrown"* (Jonah 3:4).

Wearily, he would tramp the city streets with its 750,000 souls until the people repented. With a dress indicating his prophetic office, a countenance reflecting a deep seriousness and sincerity of a man carrying a tremendous burden, and the commanding voice of a man who had been raised from the grave, his cry fell on godless ears like the tones of a loving invitation.

Behind his message and witness was the power of One who had died and was alive again; hence the reason why, as he preached, the wheels of trade slowed down, halls and haunts of sin and pleasure were deserted, and idolatry was overthrown. A great and populous city was forced to consider eternal realities. A king stepped down from his throne and begged for mercy, and all his subjects fell on their knees. Surely no other preacher has ever achieved such marvelous results in the same length of time! Well might we pray, "Do it again, O Lord!" Or pray with the prophet of old, *"Oh that thou wouldest rend the heavens, that thou wouldest come down, that the mountains might flow down at thy presence"* (Isaiah 64:1).

Perhaps we may never have the power and opportunity to make a city tremble, but we can help a penitent soul flee from the wrath to come. If we cannot cause thousands to drop on their knees, we can persuade a sinner to cry out for mercy. If we cannot convert a king, we can be the means of winning an ordinary person like Dwight L. Moody to Jesus, who in turn may win hundreds and thousands for the Master. And remember the secret that fruitful, personal soulwinning is a closer conformity to Christ in His death and resurrection.

The price of spiritual power is to be found in a daily experience of what Paul calls the power of Christ's resurrection, the fellowship of His sufferings, and the conformity to Him.[20] (See Philippians 3:10.)

Wouldst thou be a soulwinner, my friend? Then thou must live and labor on resurrection ground. When you walk and work in newness of life, you can share the risen power of Him who waits to make you a fruitful branch of the true vine.

---

20. For more on this topic, read Herbert Lockyer's book *The Price of Power.*

CHAPTER 6

THE CHALLENGE OF OUR AGE

*"Zebulun and Naphtali were a people that jeoparded their
lives unto the death in the high places of the field."*
—Judges 5:18

*"Our beloved Barnabas and Paul, men that have hazarded
their lives for the name of our Lord Jesus Christ."*
—Acts 15:25–26

We are living in an age of thrills. These are days when the spectacular doings of both sexes attract worldwide attention, bringing wealth and fame to them. Some time ago, a man risked his life in a steel barrel which went over the rapids of Niagara Falls and emerged safely in the river at Queenstown. A year or so ago in Keswick, England, an attempt was made to break the speed record on water, which resulted in the death of the owner of the ship, Sir Henry Seagrave, and his mechanic; and yet, in spite of that tragic occurrence, the boat was reconditioned, and the stunt was reattempted elsewhere.

About the same time, two men in Toronto stepped out of a flying plane to give the crowds a thrill. One man died, and the other was severely injured. A youth in search of adventure undertook a perilous journey in the icy loneliness of the far north. His hardships drove him half mad, and he was found later by native hunters in a snow house. Upon returning to this country after a time of convalescence, he told his friends that the adventure was only for sport.

Recently, two women battered a man to death "just for fun." They wanted to experience the thrill of killing someone. We read of aviators who seek to bridge the distance between continents and perish while doing so. They are perfectly willing to have their bleached bones deserted on some foreign island. Are we not awed as we read the records of scientists who go blind, have their fingers burned to stumps, and die prematurely, all because they want to feel the thrill of discovering a remedy which may benefit a dying humanity?

So, evidently, we are living in a day when there is no apparent lack of men and women who are willing to risk their lives in hazardous tasks and attempt the impossible—to do and to dare and to die. For the sake of science and commerce and worldly fame, for the sake of riches and honor, and sometimes for the cheap applause of a crowd seeking a thrill, there are many who are ready to risk life and limb to do something spectacular. The world issues its call for volunteers to devote themselves to tasks involving danger and hardship, and there is an immediate rush to face that challenge.

THE CALL OF CHRIST

But what about Christianity and the call of Christ? For more than 2,000 years, the Lord Jesus has been sounding forth the trumpet, calling upon men and women to hazard their lives for His sake, to respond to the lure of His challenge, and to enter His soul-stirring service with its high endeavor and glorious achievements. But what response has the divine Captain met? Oh, the irony of it! For almost two millenniums, He has been waiting to evangelize the world, to implant the blessed news of emancipation through the length and breadth of a sin-bound earth. And there is still a thrill in following Christ. There are dangers and difficulties to overcome and a glorious reward at the end, not merely of worldly applause and passing fame, but the recompense of a crown that will not fade away, and laurels that will last throughout eternity.

Through the centuries, Christ has been calling men and women who are willing to become martyrs for His sake. He is ever seeking those who are willing to enter the warfare from which there is no discharge. All who enlist beneath His banner need to count the cost, for it is a call to sacrifice and to soul-throbbing experiences. Scars and sobs and sorrows are wrapped up in true discipleship.

There is enough romance and sensation and fascination to stir and satisfy the most adventurous spirit in the incomparable service of the Lord Jesus. There are kingdoms that are waiting to be conquered among the tribes in heathen darkness where the Word of salvation has not yet traveled. There are wandering Bedouins perishing by the thousands in many dreary deserts where the truth has not yet penetrated. There are head hunters of Borneo who have never heard of His name, and thousands in our own land and around our very doors who, though they are surrounded with religious privileges, are yet as spiritually blind as Hottentots. Think of the curse of the drink traffic; the trail of blasted lives and broken homes; the degrading and polluting influence of the movies; the atrocious crimes that characterize our day; the gambling scourge and kindred evils, robbing life of its purity.

What scope and high endeavor, what glorious achievement, eternal fame, and honor, are reserved for all who care to cast their lives upon the altar! But what a miserable response the challenge of the divine Captain receives as He urges us on into a holy crusade against darkness of sin. He cries, "*Whom shall I send, and who will go for us?*" (Isaiah 6:8), and apart from a few souls whose hearts respond to the thrill, His call to heroism and abandonment of life in the greatest of all causes falls on deaf ears. And yet there is that which calls forth all the bravery and courage in the ardent service of the Lord Jesus that the most valiant and strongest care to give.

There is no need for us to turn to history or the many realms of our own day for illustrations of the lengths to which men and women will go in order to achieve their object. We do not dispar-age for one moment the magnificent achievement of high-spirited souls as they risk their lives in some worthy cause. What we want to do is to put in a plea for the Bible and for church history—these annals of the brave—for they can supply all the fuel we need to feed the flame of enthusiasm for truth and righteousness. If only some who are daring enough in other spheres, but absolute cow-ards where Christ and conscience are concerned, would do a little more for God, they would be manlier than they are.

THE CALL OF BIBLE GIANTS

Take the Word of God, this infallible Book! If you want thrills and soul-absorbing stories, and deeds that almost take one's breath away, you have them in God's most Holy Word—the story of Joseph in the pit and in the palace; David conquering the mighty giant; the youth in the fiery furnace at Babylon; Daniel among the lions.

And when you turn to the New Testament, you find that the sensational is pulsating in every vein. There are incidents and sto-ries in this part of the Holy Writ that make our nerves tingle every time we read them. What a heartthrob the Virgin Mary must have experienced when the angel announced the stupendous message that she was to be the mother of the world's Savior! Think of the thrill John the Baptist experienced when he defied Herod and his evil-minded mistress, and was thrown into prison! Think, too, of the thrill that Jesus realized as the common people crowded around Him and drank in His messages, and how the Pharisees withered up under His scathing rebuke! Think of how He must have felt when, in agony on the cross, He laid hold of the devil's kingdom and shouted in triumph as He died, *"It is finished"* (John 19:30)!

You who believe in honoring the brave, what plaudits and praises do you cast at the feet of Him who died and rose again for lost sinners? Oh, my friend, have you lost the thrill, the spirit of willingness to do and dare for the sake of the Lord Jesus? If you have no ambition to serve Christ, then I urge you to look back on the grim shadows of Calvary.

You may have the same sensations that stir the heart when you read the thrilling book of Acts, where men and women were willing to hazard their lives for the sake of the Lord Jesus. What enthusiasm and abandonment and willingness they showed in risking their lives and their all for the sake of Christ and the gospel! Peter was flung into prison and miraculously delivered! Saul of Tarsus was thrillingly converted upon the Damascus road and then made to step out after the Christ who saved him and to suffer indescribable agonies for His sake.

THE CALL OF BIBLE PROPHECY

When you think of the panorama of the future, it is loaded with thrills! Christ bursting through the clouds; the dead in Christ raised by the power of the Lord; the living changed; the church caught up; the rise of the antichrist; and the rise of anti-Christian forces on the earth after the removal of the church, gathering together hordes of the godless against the Lord and His anointed ones. Then will come the dramatic appearance of the Lord Jesus on earth; the turning of the moon into blood; the view of the great white throne; the destruction of death and hell; the complete revolution of the heavens and the earth; and then the surrender of a perfect kingdom by the Savior to the Father. Thrills? They abound in the Book!

Then when it comes to church history, what do we have? Why, an illustrious line of men and women who were willing to climb "the steep ascent to heaven, through peril, toil, and pain."[21] Do you not find yourself deeply moved as you meditate upon the record of martyrs, covenanters, and pioneer missionaries blazing a trail at infinite cost through some dark region for the Savior?

I am reminded of the story of Margaret Wilson, the girl of eighteen summers who had signed her name to the covenant, declaring that she would serve God according to the dictates of her conscience. Soldiers were rounding together those who had affixed their signatures to the covenant, eventually coming across young Margaret Wilson. They snatched her away from home, took her to Solway Firth, and made her fast to a mast embedded in the sands. Gradually, the tide came in, covering her shapely form, and as the waters rose and rose, the enemies behind on dry land called upon Margaret to recant and deny the covenant. But she remained silent. When the water reached her throat, they called upon her for the last time to deny the covenant and say she was sorry. If she would but respond and overthrow the covenant, they would row out, set her free, and save her from a watery grave. With the water commencing to lap around her chin, Margaret Wilson cried out, "Never! I am Christ's—let me go!"

Do you think that when John and Betty Stam were led out that day to die in China, they walked behind those men who were thirsting for their blood as a pair of miserable cowards? A thousand times, no! But with brave hearts, heads lifted up, and a firm step, they went out to suffer for their Lord, dying in triumph.

DIVINE HEROISM NEEDED

The next time you find yourself hoarse as you shout at a baseball game and yet struck dumb when you come to a prayer meeting, when you find yourself brave and courageous insofar as sport

---

21. Reginald Heber, "The Son of God Goes Forth to War," 1812.

and business are concerned and yet weak-kneed and faint-hearted for Christ's sake and cause, recall the annals of the brave and meditate on them.

Beloved, we have lost the thrill of Christian living! It has become too drab and commonplace, uneventful, artificial, superficial, and matter-of-fact. We do not have the spirit of the men of the Old Testament, who jeopardized their lives on the high places of the field; nor the passion of Barnabas and Paul as they risked their lives for the sake of the name of the Lord Jesus. We are too cold and heartless and passionless. Lethargy, indifference, and lack of zeal characterize us this day. There is no sensation in being a Christian nowadays. We serve God far too cheaply. We are not lured by the heroic and sacrificial life to which Jesus calls us. The average professing Christian has no more enthusiasm for Christ, no willingness to do and to dare and to experience the thrill and fascination of serving Him absolutely and entirely, than a tomtit. There are plenty of frills but no thrills, plenty of talk but no dramatic action, plenty of religion but no passion.

How can we recover the thrill that this exalted life calls us to? How can we get the old-time throb that these men who gave their lives for Christ experienced? Well, it seems to me that we must learn how to lose ourselves in the will of God. We must seek a deep and ever-deepening experience of power of Him who lays hold of all that we are and have, and use it in His sweet, joyful service. We must trust Him to deliver us from fear. We must fling our reputation to the winds. We must make ourselves a nuisance to the devil, until every devilish nuisance is abolished.

The cause of our weakness and cowardice, and our lack of heroic attempt and enthusiasm in the service of the Lord, is this: We have no constant contact with Him who is the source of all true heroism. If only our lives could be swayed by the Victor of Calvary and the empty tomb, then we would have self-sacrifice, zeal, and ardor that cause angels to envy us. We must live nearer to the heroic Christ Himself. Would it not cause some commotion where our lot is cast if we could live as Jesus would have us live? If sinners could see us regulating all our habits by the principles of the Sermon on the Mount, they would take notice. But the fact of the matter is that we have no thrill in serving Christ these days, for we are not separated enough from the pleasures and pursuits of this world.

DENIAL OF SELF REQUIRED

God pity you, my friend, if you can spend more money on smokes than on souls; if you can waste your time and dollars gazing at the fictitious tragedies portrayed upon the screen of today and never feel the pang of Christ over doomed souls; or if you can sacrifice your time and money and work for sport and yet never give a cent or have a desire to help the Lord accomplish His plan for the groaning world.

Not only must we live near to Christ and be baptized with His passion and compassion for the lost, but we must abandon ourselves to the sway of the Holy Spirit. It was the lordship and the presidency of the Holy Spirit in the days of the early church that produced plenty of thrills; as, for example, when Ananias and Sapphira dropped dead after acting a lie. Then the Holy Spirit enabled men to hazard their lives for the sake of the Lord Jesus and to turn the world upside down. What lengths the apostles went in dying terrible deaths for the Savior they loved!

And the world still waits for Spirit-possessed souls, for men and women who are willing to risk their lives for Christ's sake. The hour is late, and we are living in the Saturday night of the world's history. The eternal Sabbath is about to dawn, and I pray that while the lamp of life burns on, it may burn more brightly for every one of us, in His sweet, happy service. And with the Spirit's blessing on us, may we thrust in the sickle and reap. Shall we, dare we, respond to the clarion call for self-sacrifice, and fling ourselves with alacrity and gladness upon the altar, knowing, thereby, what it is to be taken up by the Holy Spirit and used to accomplish the divine purpose in the world?

"THE HAZARD"

I love the man who dares to face defeat
And risk a conflict with heroic heart.
I love the man who bravely does his part
When right and wrong in bloody battle meet.
When bugles blown by cowards sound retreat,
I love the man who grasps his sword again
And sets himself to lead his fellow men
Far forward through the battle's din and heat.

For he who joins the issue on life's field
Must fully know the hazard of the fray,
And dare to venture ere he hope to win;
Must choose the risk and then refuse to yield
Until the sunset lights shall close the day
And God's great city let the victors in.[22]

---

22. Ozora S. Davis, "The Hazard."

ABOUT THE AUTHOR

When Dr. Herbert Lockyer (1886–1984) was first deciding on a career, he considered becoming an actor. Tall and well-spoken, he seemed a natural for the theater. But the Lord had something better in mind. Instead of the stage, God called Herbert to the pulpit, where, as a pastor, a Bible teacher, and the author of more than fifty books, he touched the hearts and lives of millions of people.

Dr. Lockyer held pastorates in Scotland and England for twenty-five years. As pastor of Leeds Road Baptist Church in Bradford, England, he became a leader in the Keswick Higher Life Movement, which emphasized the significance of living in the fullness of the Holy Spirit. This led to an invitation to speak at Moody Bible Institute's fiftieth anniversary in 1936. His warm reception at that event led to his ministry in the United States. He received honorary degrees from both the Northwestern Evangelical Seminary and the International Academy in London.

In 1955, he returned to England, where he lived for many years. He then returned to the United States, where he spent the final years of his life in Colorado Springs, Colorado, with his son, Rev. Herbert Lockyer Jr., a Presbyterian minister who eventually became his editor.